Cold Call Like A Comedian

Copyright © 2019 by Brendon Lemon

Published 2019 by Kwiggz-Cortez Publishing LLC

Cover design by Kwiggz-Cortez Publishing LLC

Cold Call Like A Comedian is a work of fiction. Any resemblance to actual events, places, incidents or persons, living or dead is entirely coincidental.

All Rights Reserved.

No part of this book may be used or reproduced in any manner whatsoever without the express written permission of the publisher, except for the use of brief quotations in a book review.

COLD CALL LIKE A COMEDIAN

By Brendon "Hammer Of The Gods" Lemon

*Yeah, this album is dedicated
To all the teachers that told me I'd never amount to nothin'
To all the people that lived above the buildings that I was hustlin' in front of
Called the police on me when I was just tryin' to make some money to feed my daughter...*

It's all good baby baby

INTRO

Hey you reader! Let me start by introducing myself, I'm a stand-up comedian, but I'm also the director of North American sales development for a major digital marketing company based in Chicago.

Part of what got me to where I am in the world of sales are lessons I've learned in the 16 years I've spent in comedy. I worked my way up from actually knocking on doors for work when I couldn't get a job out of college (stand-up wasn't paying the bills), to holding a directorship and leading a team of sales development reps, teaching skills I've learned doing comedy to my sales team to help them win meetings and bring in new accounts to our sales pipeline.

Throughout this book, I'm going to share those same lessons with you and lay out strategies you can use to kick a ton of butt cold-calling, cold-email prospecting, and developing conversations that result in sales - all tied to takeaways and techniques I've come to learn from comedy.

I'm going to walk you through challenges I've faced on stage —"bombing" (telling a joke that gets no laughter), winning over crowds, flipping audiences from cold to hot—and show you how I've translated gaining trust and attention on stage to doing the same in a business setting.

My sales development teams and I have generated millions of dollars in business for the companies I've worked with in the digital marketing and manufacturing industries. I've also designed sales systems for real estate companies, manufacturing ERP software, and MarTech SaaS platforms. All of these accomplishments I've made in sales, though, have been on the back of lessons I learned in front of live audiences and the school of hard knocks as a stand-up and improv comedian.

If you want to win in sales by developing emails that have your prospects laughing out of their chairs and grabbing the phone to call you back, delivering questions and pitches like punchlines in conversations to change your prospects' minds about working with you, and altogether having a great time in your day job, this is the book for you.

I'm going to illustrate how you can find the fun in sales development and use that energy not only to enjoy yourself, but to be successful, set more meetings, and win new business. My philosophy is: if you're not having fun, then whatever you're doing isn't worth it. What I've also discovered, especially in sales, is that if you're not having fun, you're not going to make money.

This is not a book about how to succeed in comedy—I'm not going to teach you how to get booked in the comedy scene, how to be offered paid gigs, or even how to write a joke. I *am* going to teach you how to create sales material or "bits" that parallel jokes in stand-up comedy, but are entirely focused on business, sales, and early pipeline sales development. Bits in sales include: the language you use in cold emails, your talking points for cold calls, the script you use when leaving voicemails for your prospects, how you work your qualification conversations with inbound leads. If you develop effective and fun bits, you'll be more successful building trust with prospects that result in real dollars.

In this book, you'll learn:
- How to flip a cold call into a warm one

- How to become *the kind of person* that prospects want to talk with
- How to bounce back from failure with laughter and keep going
- How to stay motivated during 100-dial calling blocks
- How to organize your time and space to maximize your quality of work
- How to win over prospects with a laugh
- How to become flexible on the phone by ditching lame phone scripts
- What to show in the first 10 seconds of a phone call that will increase your success rate tenfold

So I won't be teaching you how to get a show on Netflix, but I will teach you skills to help you get a conversation going with a Netflix decision-maker to pitch your idea!

Whether you're also a comedian or performer, or if you're just here to hone new tools solely for sales, I know firsthand that the techniques in this book will help you fill out your company's pipeline with millions of dollars in business.

WHY COMEDY SALES?

Flipping a Cold Call

Let's dive right in and talk about cold-calls and the concept of "flipping" in comedy. In stand-up, flipping is what comedians do to warm up the room at the beginning of their sets, whether they're the first comic up or they're taking over the crowd's attention from the host or another act. At first glance, this might not seem like it has a lot to do with cold calling, but there are a lot of similarities between flipping an audience from the stage and gaining the right kind of attention in a cold call.

In a cold call, your audience is the person on the other end of the phone—your prospect—who you're trying to develop a relationship with. You need to get enough of your prospects' time and consideration so that they're actually listening to what you have to say when you pitch them your product or service. You need to offer them something positive—delight, interest, relief—to hold their attention and make them want to give you even more of their time, and potentially some of their colleagues' time, in the form of a formal meeting.

Comedians do this all the time; they get up on stage in front of an audience who doesn't know them, and they talk about concepts and tell jokes they've prepared beforehand. If the audience members like what a comedian has to say, they laugh. It's humor, charm, surprise, and other positive feelings that the comedian invokes that allows her to build into more material and continue to hold the room.

In comedy, you need to get a laugh about every 12 to 20 seconds. Any longer than that and the audience is going to start to turn. The same is true with a prospect on a cold call—you have only a handful of seconds at the top of a call or the first sentence of an email to get and hold your prospect's attention.

So how do comedians do this? They step up to the front of the stage, give off positive energy, and stay solid in their frame. The term "frame" here refers to a concept from the field of neuro-linguistic programming, the study of how language interacts with the brain. In neuro-linguistics, a frame is the context in which the mind receives incoming data—in other words, a frame is the setting, method, tone, etc., of how a piece of information is presented to the brain.

Let's take an example. Say you're out walking and someone comes up to you asking for money. Depending on how the person's appearance, body language, word choice, and overall demeanor, you might dismiss him or her very quickly with a, "Look, sorry, I don't have any change."

But what if that person is clean, dressed nicely, perhaps carrying a crying child? What if he says, "Hey, I just locked myself out of my car, do you have any change for me to buy my son a water and use the phone at the drugstore up the street?" The request is still the same, but your response might be completely different, because the context, the *frame*, is different.

So a successful comedian has to hold a frame in front of the audience, but instead of a frame of need and helplessness like in the example, a comedian will hold a frame of leadership. The best comedians are the best leaders; they're able to lead the audience down a train of thought they've worked out before, to conclusions they've already drawn—setups and punchlines.

Dave Chappelle, Jerry Seinfeld, and Chris Rock all do this. Chris Rock especially is an ace at framing, and I encourage you to watch his special "Bigger and Blacker." It's a masterpiece of leadership and salesmanship because Chris Rock continually takes the audience through a premise to a predetermined end, and adeptly gets buy-in every step of the way. This is what an effective comic does, and what a good sales development rep has to do over the phone or in an email.

Good sales is about good leadership, and good leadership requires you to hold a solid, confident frame with your audience—that is, with your prospects. As a leader, you set the tone for the way things are going around you, you hold the frame for how people feel around you, how they listen to and react to you. When you control the frame, you control the conversation.

Comedians learn how to be good leaders through practice, which is really a process of trial and error. They get up on stage day after day and work out bits that often don't get laughs at first. They bomb, fail, and even get booed by the audience.

Writing good material is necessary, but it's not enough. Successful comics have to figure out how to *deliver* their material in a way that works. They need to find an authentic voice and energy, and be comfortable with themselves in order to let the audience feel comfortable. In other words, great comedians have to effectively construct and hold a frame of leadership on stage.

It's taken me almost 20 years to find this in my own stand-up act. I've been on stage so much that I've grown comfortable with it, and it's become easier to find my frame. I've been through bombing and succeeding alike, almost to the point where I've become detached from the outcome I'm trying to produce, i.e. get a big laugh. This helps take the pressure off of the end goal and allows me to step into the role of a leader, and focus on my presence and relationship with the audience.

You can do this yourself in much less time though, by making the decision right now to accept what it took me nearly 20 years to learn: You can't *control* your audience, your prospect, so don't try. Instead, focus on being loose and fun with yourself, nailing your pitch, your bits, your jokes, and the rest will follow. That's leadership. Lead yourself first, then your prospects.

IT'S ABOUT CONFIDENCE

Ethos

When I've seen new comedians fail it's had less to do with the *content* of their bits, their jokes, and more to do with their level of confidence on stage. Yes, you're trying to get the audience to laugh, but the audience's laughter is meaningless to how you feel about yourself. If you're self-conscious, doubtful or critical, that comes through in your performance.

In the case of sales development, it's important to take this lesson in spades. You *don't* need to get someone to buy from you. What you're trying to do is develop a relationship from scratch with your prospect. The most successful way to do that is by being pleasant, comfortable with yourself, and confident. Be the kind of person someone wants to read, listen to, or talk with; that's the concept of ethos.

About 2,400 years ago in the 4th century BC, Aristotle wrote a book called "Rhetoric" where he explained that there are three things any communicator must produce in order to be convincing: ethos, pathos, and logos.

Briefly, I'll explain each of these. Ethos is where we get the word "ethics" from. Basically it means "character" in Greek. Pathos is where we get the word "pathetic" from; it means "emotions." Finally, "logos" is where we get the word "logic" from, and translates to "the word." Logos means *what* you're saying, pathos means *how* you're saying it, and ethos means *who you are* while saying anything.

Most books on sales focus on logos and pathos, and discuss how to refine the way you present facts and statistics (logos), and how to inject pathos in the form of emotion and transference of emotion to get someone to set a meeting or sign a contract. Many sales techniques involve "buying pressure" or leveraging fear, uncertainty, or doubt to drive conversations.

The problem is this: in early pipeline sales, if you insert fear, uncertainty, or doubt into your messages, prospects will ignore you, avoid you, and hang up on you. Nobody wants to be scared by an email or made to feel doubtful in a phone conversation with a perfect stranger.

"Hey, this is Brendon calling from Dynamic Works. Did you know your website shows four common risk factors that are exposing you to—" Click. That's about where the prospect decides to end the conversation.

There are two reasons why that opening line in a cold call is unproductive: First, it's presenting too much data for the prospect's brain to process on the fly. In other words, the logos—the actual content of the message—is inappropriate for a first conversation with a new person. Second, it's immediately threatening in tone, theme, and presentation.

"Ethic" actually translates to "morality" or "character" in Greek. In sales, you want to develop the kind of character that makes people want to interact with you. Ask yourself, "What can I do, who can I be, *how* can I behave in a way that will get people interested to talk to *me*?"

The famous comedian Bernie Mac said, "When I go on stage, I want to relieve your mind, your pressures." This is true in comedy, and it's true in sales development. You need to be the kind of person who has something refreshing and interesting to say—and it doesn't have to be solely about *your* business, *your* core offering, or something *you* want your prospects to buy.

In fact, establishing relationships in early pipeline sales is not really about *you*, the salesperson—it's about your prospects. What are their interests? What are their companies' goals? What's engaging to them? What can you say that will stimulate the spark in your prospects' minds to give you their attention and allow you to deliver a value prop to them?

Comedians gauge the answers to similar questions when they "read" the crowd. They pick up on the amount and tenor of laughs at the beginning of a set, and they use that information to determine what bits, tags, and punchlines will be most effective at drawing in the audience. As a sales development rep, your audiences usually consist only of a single person, so you can do more tailored research, which we'll discuss later, and really home in on selling yourself to each individual prospect.

Any comedian who's been on stage enough and bombed enough knows: you have to sell yourself first and establish a rapport with your audience. Sales development is no different. You have to be enthusiastic, comfortable, and confident when you engage with your prospects. In early pipeline sales, your personality and demeanor is more important than selling your product or service. If you sell yourself first, you can more effectively sell your company later.

Assignment 1: Personal Qualities

Write three qualities you have that make you valuable and worthwhile in a conversation. Focus on your personal characteristics rather than your sales proposition, product or service offering, or company. Here are some questions to consider when identifying these qualities:

- What unique thing(s) have you done recently or in the past?
- What intriguing facts or ideas do you have to offer?
- What traits set you apart from other people at a party or social event?
- What research or statistics do you know that would impress a stranger?
- What passion or interest do you pursue outside of the office?
- What makes your friends appreciate your company?

For example, an answer to the last question might be that you're a good listener (a critical skill we'll discuss cultivating later in this book), or that you always have a bright, optimistic outlook on their challenges or struggles. There are many possible answers and many directions you can go here! Take a few minutes to brainstorm, then jot down your three qualities.

THE COMEDIAN'S MINDSET

Introduction

Let's discuss something that's been very important to my success both on stage and in sales development, something I call "The Comedian's Mindset." This is a mode of thinking I've recognized in myself over my many years doing stand-up. As time goes on, I've noticed myself operating in this same mindset in the world of sales development. In fact, the more I've been able to consciously or unconsciously leverage the Comedian's Mindset in sales, the more positive the results I've realized.

In my reflections on how comedians succeed and how and why stage methods translate to sales, I've come across a handful of key lessons that together make up the Comedian's Mindset.

The Comedian's Mindset: Failure

First thing to gaining The Comedian's Mindset is to accept what every seasoned comedian already knows: you're going to fail.

Failure is the one thing you need to accept *will* happen to you. While others shy away from and try to avoid it at all costs, you must become best friends with it. The attitude that failure is not an option actually creates unnecessary frustration, stress, and anxiety, all of which exhibit themselves physically in your body and behavior. Negative emotions betray themselves in your voice, in the way you move, and even in the thoughts and words you employ as you speak.

If you've ever broached a topic on the phone with a prospect and then backed away from it, consider why that might have happened. Were you feeling pressure to succeed? Did your prospect give pushback or indicate disinterest in your conversation? Your act of abandoning the topic for fear of failure not only precluded any possible success, but also undermined your confidence and conveyed low status to your prospect.

This goes back to the concept of the frame and ethos. There's a fine line between establishing rapport with your audience or prospect, and allowing that rapport, or lack of it, to drive your own behavior. If sales and comedy are both about leadership, then your indication that the audience's, or prospect's, interests and well-being are *more important* than your material or value prop shows poor leadership and low value. People don't want to follow low-value leaders, so if you're trying to sell something, you must convey that you and your product are valuable. And the best way to do that is by *believing* it.

Comedy and sales development are not a commodities exchange—they're ultimately a business of selling value. You must realize that failure is part of the process and that you'll live through it before you can truly succeed.

In Improv comedy, the one thing that kills a scene, an improv, the fastest is when the players begin feeling the fear of failure. Fearing failure, and avoiding it, causes performers to start playing a small game—a game to *not lose*, rather than a game *to win*. Of course, in this case "winning" is having fun and giving the audience a lot of delight.

I started doing stand-up when I was 16 years old, and was actually cursed for the first year I did comedy because I was too successful! I started at Mark Ridley's Comedy Castle in Detroit, and for months every time I got on stage I'd consistently win over the audience and get laughs, so much so that Mark "passed" me. In the comedy world, being "passed" at a club or venue is a pretty big deal—it means you can go up whenever you want at that particular stage.

The problem was that I'd never dealt with failure. About a year into doing comedy, I bombed really hard one night. I didn't get a single laugh, and the audience was entirely unenthused about me and my material. To add insult to injury, I was on a first date that night! To this day, I have no idea what happened, which is something fairly common in the stand-up scene and the world of sales development.

Sometimes crowds aren't with you and don't find your jokes funny. Sometimes your prospect hangs up on you or turns up to a meeting no longer interested in your product. In all of these cases, you may never know the real reason why.

And while it's important to attempt to understand the barriers to your success, actions that have resulted in failure in the past, it's equally as important to understand that there are some things outside of your control.

You're going to fail. Even if you have a great run, eventually failure catches up to you.

The acceptance of failure as something outside of your control, as something that's dependent not on you but on someone else, is paramount to your ability to get the job done and be the kind of person that other people want to talk and listen to. As a comedian, if you have expectations that the audience will laugh at very particular places in your set and respond specifically to parts of your material, the audience members will feel that pressure and become uncomfortable and unwilling to laugh.

It's similar in sales development. As soon as you release your prospect from your own expectations of being a certain way or responding to you in a specific manner, then they will have some comfort and ease to continue to speak with you, even if they ultimately won't buy what you're offering.

The way to view failure is to just consider it feedback. If someone hangs up on you, if you're not advancing conversations in ways that lead to opportunities and new business, think about those outcomes as simple feedback. You might not be doing a good job, so accept it. People who are in training to become pros or experts have to miss and fail a lot on the process of honing their skills for the future—and they'll probably still fail at least a little, even when they've reached higher levels in their area of practice. Failure can never be wrong if you think of it as a natural part of your process.

So try out some new things often, and fail quickly. Most comedians try out jokes sometimes hundreds of times before they cut them; they really try to believe in their material. Comedians try out material until they internalize it, until it becomes a part of them.

What you want to foster is an organic, conversational way of approaching a prospect. You want to understand what you're planning on saying, your talk tracks. You want to practice and internalize an elevator pitch (we'll go through elevator pitch a bit later). You want to understand how to talk without being reliant on delivering a specific script because if you're too rigid you'll lose flexibility and be stilted in your speech, losing the confidence of your prospect.

If you can't speak organically, naturally, you'll have a lot of pressure internally to make sure you're saying the words of your script, and you won't be able to handle real-time feedback from your prospect. This will lead to a strange feeling for both you and the prospect, and because you don't have a rapport with them it becomes very easy for them to turn off.

So the first thing you want to do is make sure that you're organic, comfortable, and natural, and to do that you must accept failure and not avoid it. You want to accept that you don't have control over what your prospect does. Once you've accepted these things with yourself, you're actually inviting your prospect to feel comfortable with you because you're feeling comfortable with yourself.

The Comedian's Mindset: Positive State, Positive Feelings

The mindset that's successful for sales development is simple, it's a positive state and positive feelings. Basically, if you want to succeed, you're going to have to have a good time.

A big switch flipped in my mind when I was doing comedy and realized, "Oh, if I'm not having a good time on stage then nobody else in this room is going to either."

To be a successful comedian I have to lead the audience to the things that I enjoy and I find fun. Even though comedians sometimes talk about depressing things or things that are sad—"Oh, my girlfriend left me, I got fired from my job, I'm getting older" and other things like this—they're trying to find the fun in those subjects and they're inviting the audience to share in the fun they're discovering. If a comedian is not having a good time while they're on stage then the audience is not going to buy into anything the comic is doing and nobody is ever going to like them.

There's an old phrase in sales that "First you sell yourself." This is true, and having The Comedian's Mindset is the best way to approach selling yourself.

What you have to do is ensure that you, as the sales rep, are actually having a great time while you're on the phone. You need to do whatever you need to do to make that happen. For every person reading this book it's going to be something different. You have to discover for yourself what gets you in a good mood.

For me, getting into a good mood for prospecting starts in the morning with a little meditation; I sit quietly for ten to twenty minutes after I wake up. When I get to work, I get into a good mood by challenging myself to create a Flow state while I call and email. I set time in two hour blocks that I use to organize my activity, going back and forth from 20 minutes of work and then 5 to 10 minutes of a break. I track how many calls I make and how many emails I send every hour just to see if I'm at a good work pace. I go from one call to the next. I turn off my email software. I focus only on calls. I play music in the background to get myself pumped up. I pause the music whenever I make a call. I make the call, I hang up the phone, then put the music back on. I take some notes, I get to the next call. This is my routine and it works for me, you have to figure this out for yourself.

A really important thing to note here is that if you get into a place where you're in a bad mood while prospecting then you need to stop. More than anything else, early pipeline sales is driven by personality and character, and if you're not the kind of person someone wants to talk to then no one's going to want to talk to you. This is just the case. If you're sad, if you're negative, if you're having a bad day, either figure out a way to get out of that state and into a pleasant place where you're able to offer positive energy and positive feelings to your prospects or schedule another time to do it.

If you have a good manager, they're going to understand that sometimes you're just not able to deliver. If you're a good SDR then your manager will know that you're putting in effort, and sharing your feelings comes from a place of honest disclosure. You're saying, "Look, I can't do it today. I'm not feeling up to it. I'm not going to be valuable to anybody on the phone, and I just need to take a break." Go for a walk, listen to other music, call your mother or father, call your girlfriend or boyfriend, and get back in state. Do whatever you have to do to basically appreciate the opportunity that you have and then get back in the hot seat and deliver.

Once you realize again that you have something valuable to contribute, to sell, and that *you* are someone valuable to others, then get back on the phone and start doing it again.

The reason prospects will hang up if they sense negatives feelings on you is because the human brain is wired at a basic level to understand if something is pleasurable or painful. Is it a threat or an opportunity? It's one or the other. From a prospect's perspective, the littlest bit of indication that the call they picked up could be painful or negative is going to cause them to turn defensive and most likely hang the phone up.

This is the reason why fear, uncertainty, and doubt doesn't work in early prospecting calls; you don't have enough rapport with someone to trust that you're not a threat to them. To them, you're a stranger. What you have to do very early is continue to offer value by being a positive and non-threatening person and generate enough rapport to be critical of what they're currently doing.

Rather than trying to inject fear, uncertainty and doubt right off the bat in a phone call, build some rapport, maybe set a quick meeting for later, and *then* say: "Hey look, now that we've been talking for a few minutes and we have a meeting on the calendar, I want to let you know I actually did an analysis of your web presence and I can tell you that you're not secure, you're leaving yourself exposed to threats and I really need to show you those because I actually care about your web presence and your well-being." Getting your prospect's continued buy-in is only possible if you've generated enough rapport early to be able to say this.

Scientific studies have shown that negative emotions have a fivefold impact over positive emotions. For you, this means that if you inspire one negative emotion, you have to overcome that

5x with positive emotions in order for your prospect to actually feel good about continuing to speak with you. This shows us that you really do need to offer lots and lots of value early through positive presence by being fun and having fun. So figure out what process works for you and get into state, that way you can offer positive emotions both over the phone and over email.

The Comedian's Mindset: The Grind

The third thing in the Comedian's Mindset lesson is The Grind. Every comedian understands what the grind is.

Comedians go from open mic to open mic to open mic to show to show to show. When a comedian is getting up in front of audiences all the time, that's called "the grind." Every comedian knows it; you do the same material in front of different audiences all over the place, in Los Angeles, Chicago, New York, Denver, Houston, any major city. Sometimes comedians go from show to show, telling jokes in front of audiences night after night, time after time, sometimes three, four, five, even six or more times in a single evening.

Why go through this kind of masochism? It allows comedians to work out their bits and material. The grind let's them practice their material. They can try out new material, they practice old material, they get in front of audiences and gain more experience, you get good feedback on the things that you do, and also you get exposure that could lead to bigger opportunities. Many times comedians are booked for gigs because they're seen at another show or an open mic.

When comedians go from gig to gig, they aren't going with the intention of trying to *get* something from the show—not going just to make *this* audience laugh, to get a specific opportunity, to try to get on SNL, to audition for something; they're actually going just to get the experience for themselves. So, if they get up in front of a crowd and fail, it doesn't really matter. Remember, they're grinding, there's four other mics that they're going to that night, there's two other shows that they're doing that evening. They have more opportunities to get up and succeed.

Using The Grind mindset is the way to approach sales development. Try to see that performing well as a comedian comes as a result of performing a lot. The same is true about making cold calls: It isn't about *this* call, it's about *calls*. It's not about *this* email, it's about *emails*.

It's important to attempt to do well every time, but you need to *relieve* yourself from the burden of trying to make something happen. It *feels* like it's important to make something happen because getting *a* pickup when cold calling feels like a limited opportunity. This is an abundant world, and there's going to be more people for you to go after to make business happen. You'll set more meetings and you'll make more money more often if you look at your outreach through the lens of The Grind.

Every day, I punch the clock as a comedian and get up in front of as many people as I can, as often as I can, to try and work out my bits and improve myself. The same is true with sales development. If you're trying to work out an elevator pitch, the best way to do it is to sit down and work on it for a minute, but then get on the phone and try it in the real world. Make a dozen or ten dozen phone calls, and by the end of that your elevator pitch is going to be far more rock-solid than if you spent the same amount of time just working on your elevator pitch.

You might say to yourself, "What happens if I fail and I burn a 120 different phone calls?" The answer to the question is this: it doesn't matter.

Most comedians get back up in front of those same audiences the next day, or the next week, or the next month and they do the *same* jokes, but they've gotten better. The truth is that your prospects have so many things going on in their lives that they're not going to think about you, so you'll have *another* opportunity to get up another time and do better at that time. And actually, if they do remember you, they might even respect it.

So think about that; it's a grind. Comedy is a result of paying attention to the outcome while focusing on the performances and the process. Sales from sales development, conversations that lead to sales, come from a result of focusing on trying to do well each time while accepting that you only have so much you can do. Focus on the process and continuing to move the process forward.

Grind.

The Comedian's Mindset: Yes, And

The fourth lesson is "Yes, And." Maybe some of you reading this have taken improv and you've heard of this rule. 'Yes, And' is a foundational rule of improv; it means building and not denying.

Now, why does it work? It works because the comedians who do improv co-create an improv scene with other improvisers by making up a narrative together. By each adding a little bit together, bit-by-bit, they build a scene together in front of an audience in real time. The way improvisers do that is by building on elements that other improv comedians have already introduced in the scene.

The process of "Yes, And" functions similarly to the way rapport is built between people. Denying someone, or throwing up a "No," is rapport destroying. There's nothing inherently wrong with destroying rapport; in your life with many of the people who you interact with that's probably fine to do. You probably share a laugh. With your friends, whom you've known for a long time, you actually have a lot of rapport. The problem is that when you're trying to connect with people who you've never spoken with before, throwing up negativity and destroying rapport harms your ability to create a real relationship early.

To be clear, when I say, "Throwing up a boundary early," I mean in the first few moments of meeting someone, in the first few seconds of talking with someone on the phone. You haven't known this prospect for more than maybe 30 seconds, if you start throwing up boundaries too early, or you break rapport too much it's going to induce negative feelings because they're going to feel a barrier and it's not going to feel positive to them at all. That's not why they came to speak with you, and it certainly isn't something that they want to get from someone who is trying to speak to them.

The last thing I would want to hear as the recipient of a cold-call from someone I don't know is that I'm doing something wrong or bad or something I said isn't good, or anything like that. I would hang up immediately. The caller doesn't know me, they don't know who I am, I have no rapport with them, and the last thing I want is to have anybody speaking negatively to me if they don't know me. I don't need that kind of negativity in my life and neither does any of the high-value people you're trying to connect with; so keep that in mind.

Luckily, the way you side-step this in conversation with a prospect is actually pretty simple: you don't deny.

So if a prospect throws up something at you like, "Hey, you know what, sorry. We already have a vendor, and we don't need to speak with you." Don't say, "Oh wait. No, you don't have a vendor. You do need to speak with us because blah-blah-blah-blah-blah..." Immediately, your prospect will cut you out.

Instead, what you need to say is, "Oh man, that's so great that you already have a vendor. I'm glad that you see that this is a problem that you need a partner to solve. Let me just ask you: how's your vendor performing? Are you happy with them?"

You can easily observe the difference and *feel* it. In the second example, I tried to open the conversation up to a little bit more. I'm not going to try to deny them; I'm not going to try to get to know who their vendor is by attacking their vendor. I wouldn't try to introduce fear, uncertainty, or doubt, not yet. This is maybe the fifth second, tenth second I'm speaking with the prospect, it doesn't make any sense at all to try to break rapport with them. In the early part of the phone call, the only thing I want to do is develop a real relationship with the prospect. The way that I do that is by accepting everything they say and just simply being thrilled with it; continuously injecting positive energy.

"Oh man. I'm so happy you're talking to me. That's cool that you got a vendor. I mean, you know if there's no way that we can do business that doesn't bother me at all; it's just great to see that you also see that this is something worth handling in your company. You know let me know what else I could help you with, or maybe I can forward something else to you that would be useful, or if you want to talk about your vendor, I can maybe indicate a couple of things that I know that they maybe don't handle well. Mind if I ask, who are you speaking with over there?"

Any of those things are totally appropriate to say when you've actually accepted what your prospect is telling you. So don't deny them. And again, look at this process as a game; you're trying to co-create, collaborate together in a reality the two of you are on the phone. You're actually inviting them into the space that you're building on the phone while speaking with them. That's how a real conversation works; and the way that you develop a real relationship is by having a real conversation. If they give you a dismissal then your job is to incorporate it into the conversation. Just to be clear, a dismissal is not the same as an objection. We'll go into further detail later, but briefly, an objection is when a prospect says "Here's why we can't work together," meanwhile a dismissal is the prospect saying "I don't want to speak with you."

And there's a lot of reasons people give dismissals. They could be having lunch, they could have just come out of a meeting, they could just be having a bad day, somebody could have yelled at them moments earlier, their boss could have told them "You know, if anybody calls from email companies that want to work with us, I don't want to talk to any of them." Any of these are good dismissals, and they have nothing to do with you. So if somebody says, "Hey look, I just came out of a meeting," throw that right into your situation: "Oh, you just came out of a meeting. How'd it go?" Injecting "Yes, And" into the conversation is very simple and actually kind of fun.

If you accept what the prospect tells you and you use "Yes, And," you can deal with negative feedback. One of the things that I'm happy to do with my team is that every time somebody gets hung up on, we get very excited. We celebrate, everybody gives a high-five, we go, "Man, that was a bad call! That was not good for anybody. It wasn't good for me, it wasn't good for anybody on the phone!" We're just very excited that we could get a hangup out of the way early in the day and move on from it.

If you're able to use 'Yes, And' and have a lot of fun, you can even do something as simple and fun as emailing someone a Starbucks digital gift card and say, "Hey look, it sounds like you're having a bad day, you might need something sweet!" That is a great "Yes, And." So incorporate the feedback that you're getting from prospects on the phone, keep positive, and it always build and expand, don't deny, don't close down.

The Comedian's Mindset – Assignments

Here are the assignments for this section on The Comedian's Mindset:

1. Analyze your current sales mindset - Get a piece of paper and pen, write for five minutes and ask yourself: How you think about failure? How do you create a positive environment for yourself? How do you get in state for prospecting? How do you enjoy the time that you have while you're trying to work or while you're trying to "do" sales? Give yourself a moment to understand

what your current sales mindset is.
2. Understand how you deal with rejection - Do some journaling answering the following questions: How do you deal with rejection? Do you get hurt? Do you stop? Does it indicate to you that maybe you are in the wrong place? Do you need to take a minute, go for a walk, clear your head? What does your body do? And also, importantly, how do you get yourself motivated after rejection? How do you get yourself motivated to bounce back? Your success will be based on an intimate understanding of this.
3. Understand your power in the situation - On the same piece of paper ask yourself some of the following questions: What are things in your outreach that you can't control? Maybe it's how many prospects pick up, how their day is going, etc. What are things that you can do and that you can control? What are something you're not doing now that you can start doing to enable more sales later? Maybe it's something like "I need to keep track of my calls." Maybe you write something like "I need to send out at least 50 emails a day," or maybe "I need to get a list of people in front of me before I start calling and I need to keep track of who said what, when." There's a lot of different ways that sales development can go but accepting what you can do *now*, and then doing it, is much more productive than trying to make it up as you go along.

ORGANIZATION

Getting Ready to Attack Calls & Emails

In this section, we're going to talk a little bit about organization. We'll discuss a little about the physical preparation for prospecting, and the things required to make sure that you can sell successfully over and over in a predictable way.

In order to prospect, you need to have a lot of activities lined up for you to do. Just like in comedy, you can't grind if you don't have performances lined up. Comedians go out and they'll line up more than one open mic at a time; they'll line up three, four, sometimes more than that in a night. What they're trying to do is get in front of as many audiences as possible to get experience and refine the jokes that they're working on.

Because comedians are so organized (ironic, isn't it?), they aren't *precious* about being on stage; it's something they do often. This is the mentality you need to develop about sales calls and calling up prospects. Try to do the best job you can every time you get in front of a prospect, but don't be precious about success and not worried about failing.

To get organized, put together a list of prospects in a spreadsheet or maybe some sales enablement software like Salesloft, Outreach.io, or Hubspot. This will ensure that you're ready to move from call to call to call to call while prospecting. Grinding works because when comedians line up that many mics at a time, they don't have time to process the feelings they're having about their own material. When comedians grind, they record their sets on their phone and then they go straight to the next set at a different show. If they have a bad set they don't have time to sit down and wallow in those feelings, which would be unproductive.

Go from the next to the next to the next without pausing to review or analyze what has happened. Later, you can go back and review what you did and how you did it to take any lessons out of your activity. If possible, you should record your talk tracks (pitches, overcoming objections or dismissals, etc.).

If you live in a region that allows you to record your phone calls with prospects, you should do that to try to hear yourself. But basically, you want to open up some kind of sheet, and it doesn't have to be more sophisticated than a spreadsheet, and list off all the people you're looking to call or email and make sure that you have enough organization so that you can go from the next to the next.

Once you've organized who you're going to reach out to, now it's time to organize your schedule. I schedule two hour time blocks for prospecting that I call "2H time." Basically, two hour time blocks where you have no other focus but prospecting. Because of the focus that prospecting takes, you don't want to switch from prospecting tasks for at least two hours.

When you start a 2H time block, you'll sit down with your prospecting list ready to go with as many contacts on it as necessary to cover that two-hour time. Who knows how many that could be? It could be 30, it could be 40, but a sufficient number that will keep you busy for 120 minutes calling, leaving messages, trying to connect, reaching out to the next person, but *not* emailing.

Why not emailing? Because what you want to do is focus on *one* task at a time. You want to focus on calls, trying to connect with prospects over the phone, *or* focus on emails, not split focus between the two. For this same reason, you don't want to research and then call a prospect. Instead of switching gears between different types of tasks, which will waste time and break your Flow state (we'll discuss further, later), you want to have all the research already done and focus only on calling or only on emailing. You want to know what the next name your dialing is, and you want to know what you're going to say when that person answers the phone; that's grinding. Each comedian knows their jokes and they go from show to show knowing the next audience they can get in front of.

There are a lot of ways you can grind using 2H time, but Skype is a good VoIP provider, RingCentral is also decent, but honestly just using a cell phone works fine. Honestly, a very good office set up for prospecting, better than some that I've seen, is only a spreadsheet and a cell phone, that's all anyone really needs.

If you work in an organization currently, you probably have both inbound leads and outbound sales prospecting. What you want to focus on is outbound prospecting. This is because, hopefully, these are targets your company has decided are *most likely* worth working with before anyone has even picked up the phone to dial them. Inbound leads are people who are interested in working with your company, but the truth is that they have a lot of questions and they're actually a giant waste of time, most of the time. Whether or not inbound leads are worthwhile obviously depends on your business.

Just like calls and emails, you do not want to switch between outbound and inbound prospecting. Instead, you want to put dedicated time together to do one or the other. Mostly, you'll want to prioritize outbound prospecting in an attempt to connect with prospects on the phone, and have a conversation with them that could result in business. The most important thing is organizing your time and organizing your outreach, that's how you get things done.

Getting Into Flow, Keeping Yourself Motivated & Focused

In this section, we'll address the physical prep or the environment that you're actually working in. This is important because we discussed "2h time" in the last section; when you're going to sit down for two hours and not be interrupted while you prospect.

2H time is based slightly on something called "The Pomodoro method." So named because the person who invented it used a timer that looked like a little tomato—hence the Italian name 'Pomodoro'—and would timeout 20 to 25 minutes of time where they focused on only one task. During that time they would note down whether or not they had an interruption, and whether or not that interruption was internal or external (think having to get a drink of water vs. having a colleague tap you on the shoulder to ask a question). In either case, the principle is this: you want to limit the number of possible interruptions you could have because you're going to be focused on trying to create a Flow state.

Flow is a mental state first identified by the performance psychologist Mihaly Csikszentmihalyi (pronounced "Me-high cheek-sent-me-high), and is present in all high-performers. It's what athletes describe as "the zone." Pertinent to all performers, comedians experience this when on stage, in front of an audience, moving with the rhythms of their own comedy and the response of the audience. This is a state that anyone who wants to be successful must discover how to produce in themselves.

You want to create a Flow state when you are prospecting. Studies of people in Flow indicate that tracking yourself against time in order to be as productive as possible is a good way to get into this state. Studies show that people in Flow are 500% more productive than people in non-Flow states when working on the same activities. You can get done five times the amount of work in the same amount of time if you're focused and in a Flow state; you can look it up. This is really not a lesson on how to develop Flow, but it's important to understand why limiting interruptions is important.

So, you can't do comedy without certain bits of equipment: you need a microphone, you need a stage or at least some performance space, you need a speaker, you need a light, you need something that actually creates the environment for comedy. Once that environment is created, something special really does happen. Comedians don't get up and start talking acapella in front of groups of people in bars and call it an open mic; it's not really how comedy works. What you want to do is produce changes in your environment that make it easier for you to get into a Flow state for prospecting. The way to do it is by limiting interruptions and creating an environment that inspires you to actually become a better prospector.

So here's what you should do: you should listen to good music, you should have a notebook ready to take notes, you should actually mark off in that notebook how many calls and emails you've completed in a one-hour period of time and track yourself against them; that's fun and it creates a goal. It should inspire a little competition in yourself to beat the clock, or beat yourself, or beat your previous best, or beat your colleagues. The point is that it should actually inspire more productivity.

Make sure you're in a quiet environment. You don't want background noise coming through to your prospect. You don't want interruptions while you're on the phone. When prospects hear background chatter on your side the call they immediately think you're in a calling room and will hang up on you, so dial from a quiet location. Have some coffee, have a drink, have maybe more than one drink at hand. I always work with coffee and carbonated water just within reach; just so I have everything to be prepared and comfortable.

Have a computer but don't spend your time tooling around on the internet but instead have it ready in case you need to Google something while on the phone with a prospect. Have your CRM or tracking spreadsheet open, maybe have LinkedIn open; take a look at the different people that you're dialing and have the ability to pull information very quickly if you have to.

Comedians always have a notebook, it's their cheat sheet. Every comedian has all the jokes they're working on in there. They have their routine, they have everything spelled out in this notebook, and what I want you to have is something similar. You need to have a small sheet with notes about your pitch, what you're going to talk about, key selling points, and any research you've done on the prospects you're reaching out to. If you have one or two bits of personal information about your prospects and can place them into the conversation it *will* make a difference in how successful you are.

The basic lesson is this: control your environment. Make sure that you have everything you need so that there are no distractions. You want to lock in, you want to tighten up, and you want to go through your calls without having anything to derail you so that your brain can stay in "the zone." You don't want distraction interrupting you the same way that a comedian doesn't want hecklers interrupting him on stage. He wants his audience locked in, he wants himself locked in. I want you to do the same thing with your cold calls.

CALL STRATEGY

Have a Plan

Although it feels like comedians on TV look like they're just making it up as they go along, comedians don't just get up on stage and wing it. They have a plan. Whether they're drawing from things they've said over and over that they know they can bring out in front of an audience, or experience improvising, dealing with hundreds of audiences, they're not just making it up as they go along.

Good comedians are prepared, and so are good salespeople. You, of course, have maybe heard of improv and you're thinking "Oh, but that's just making it up, that's just ad-libbing, and yes-and-ing." Well, as somebody who's done improv for 14 years, I can tell you that you never go into an improv without something; you need a suggestion, you need a structure. Improvisers rely on something to actually carry them through the improv besides just getting up on stage and making it up.

Getting on a cold call without a proper plan is like pulling an audience member up on stage and having them try to entertain the crowd; it would never work. So, if somebody doesn't have a background, training, *a plan*, they would flounder and fall apart and it would make everyone feel uncomfortable and everything would suck before it began. So, your first step should be to have a plan.

Plans can be as simple as "I want to ask this person who handles the account," or "I want to know when their contract is up for renewal." Either of these are solid, simple plans. Usually cold calls have a goal of setting a meeting. If you have a goal of setting a meeting, know *why* you're trying to set one, what the goal of that meeting is supposed to be (note, it isn't "work with our company"), and why the prospect should be sold on taking it. If you can't answer these questions, go back to the drawing board and answer them before picking up the phone. A good way to have a plan is by getting in touch with your curiousity, and calling prospects to get answers to your questions. "Hey, I was just calling because I was wondering who your current data partner is, from my research it looked like Xylcorp, is that true? Who handles that relationship?"

Failing anything else, the plan you should have should be "I want to find the right person to talk with."

Find the Right Person Have an Agenda

At a high level, the reason you're reaching out to an organization is to try to see if there's an opportunity to do business together. It's important to understand that the opportunity to work together, to do business and make money, only lies with *people*. People have to make the decision to do business, people have to make consideration, people are the ones you need to speak with, so everything in the sales process comes *after* you have found the right person.

Now, there's a lot of ways you can find the right person. You can certainly do a lot of research, which might take hours, but the fastest and easiest way is just to call and ask, "Who's the right person I should speak with?"

You don't want to waste time with anybody who can't help you, but more importantly, you don't want to waste your time with anybody who isn't the right person. Keep this in mind: you're not actually selling anything yet. You're not selling a product, you're not selling a service, you're selling yourself and at *most* selling a conversation between you and the right person at the organization you're prospecting. Understand that at this point, there's no pressure yet; you're just trying to find the right person to have a conversation with.

If you get a lot of no's, that's totally fine, that's part of the process; it's why prospecting requires persistence. If someone you didn't know came to your house and wanted to be friends with you, you'd probably think they were a little crazy. But over time if they showed you again and again that they could be a valuable person you'd be okay with it and might end up becoming good friends with them. You're selling *that* conversation to prospects.

I can't tell you *exactly* what you need to do on your prospecting calls, but I can tell you what you shouldn't do; and that is be needy. The way to avoid being needy is by having an agenda. Before you pick up the phone, have an idea of what you're going to say and how you're going to say it, we're going to work on pitches later, but for now, you need to pick up the phone, begin dialing, and have an idea in your head of what you're actually to say when your prospect answers. That, of course, requires you to know a little bit about them; you'll have to do some research. Have to have your cheat sheet handy, you'll have to talk briefly about why you're calling and who you are and what you want. Don't force your agenda, don't be needy, don't *need* something to happen, don't push someone into the idea of doing something *you* want to do. You want them to always *elect* to do something *they* want to do.

Be open to changing your agenda in the moment. Be flexible with your goals, and with the plan of how to get a meeting. If you've connected with the right person, and you have a good message, and they have problems that lines up with what your company solves, it is literally only a matter of time before a meeting will happen with them. In other words, be patient and stay positive.

Be okay if they don't want to talk to you. You're interrupting their day. It's okay to acknowledge that. You probably sound a lot like a whole bunch of losers who call them every day and ask them for their time. Remember, they have their own agenda. You're trying to make a case that you're worth talking to and worth taking a meeting with, you could have something valuable to offer, but you look a lot like people who have wasted their time in the past.

Most prospects have internalized that someone on a cold call can hurt them because they don't know who you are and they know that you can waste their time. They need to feel that there's only upside for them in talking further with you, and the first step to doing that is to prove to them very quickly that you won't cause any harm.

How do you do that? You exercise patience, positivity, good demeanor and good character, and then you show that you've done some research. If anything happens on the call to draw them away from thinking that the conversation could be anything but potentially valuable for them, they will hang up on you. Humans are hardwired after thousands of years of evolution to be very sensitive to any feelings of discomfort from strangers. You may feel awkward or strange on the phone, its okay to feel that way, but just feel it and accept it, then move forward.

You have to be comfortable with the fact that most likely, at first, your prospects don't want to talk to you. If they say, "I'm sorry. I can't speak right now," and hang up, that's fine. You can give them a call back later, or you can email them. Being hung up on doesn't mean they don't want to talk to you *period*; it means they don't want to talk to you *right then*. So, that's something to keep in mind as well.

It's critical that your prospects feel that *they* can make the decision to move forward with you, on their own volition. That's the call strategy: patience, positivity, and letting the prospect be who they are. You don't need your prospect to be any certain kind of way or do any kind of certain thing. Once you feel this way, and internalize this call strategy, then you have a foundation to make lots and lots of successful calls.

BITS VS. SCRIPTS

Overview

"What are bits?" I can almost hear you thinking. They're similar to scripts, but the difference between scripts and bits is that in the world of comedy you don't really have a script.

Actors have scripts. Politicians who get on stage and deliver a talk typically have scripts. But scripts are too rigid for a comedian. Comedians don't do a one-man show, like a monologue. Instead, comedians have jokes which they string together into bits. They have little things they say that run together that they can drop into one place or another while speaking that fit into the moment almost like anecdotes, continuing the conversation with the audience while moving them along. That's what a bit is.

Bits are to comedians what audio samples are to a DJ, they're a handful of little talk tracks that go together: jokes, setups, punchlines, that all work toward a point. That's the idea of a bit. And they function differently than scripts. It's very important, actually, because they allow the comedian to have a conversation with the audience. Whereas a one-man show or a speech isn't a conversation, it's a monologue, comedy is a *dialogue*.

So, if you watch comedy, watch Chris Rock, watch Louis C.K., you watch these comedians, you will see what they're actually doing is having a continual conversation with the audience. They're listening to the audience's response. They're responding in kind. It's a collective conversation, but it's definitely a conversation. They're not simply delivering joke after joke; if the audience wasn't on board, they couldn't continue to do comedy. It's very important to understand this point, because it is critical in cold calls.

You need to have the consent to continue, a tacit agreement from the prospect that you're speaking with on the call to move ahead in the sales conversation with you. The way that you do that is by having bits to move the prospect forward in the conversation.

Good Listening Skills

As mentioned before, the difference between successful and unsuccessful comedians is the ability to listen. There are a lot of comedians who write good jokes, but their performances don't go anywhere because they can't listen to the audience. If the audience isn't on board at the beginning, they won't be on board at the end.

If you've ever seen a comedian bomb on stage, first of all, that must be very uncomfortable for you. I'm sorry you had to go through that. But, the reason they bombed is always the same: they failed to listen to and appropriately respond to the audience. They either didn't have the tools, meaning the jokes, the bits, the talk tracks, to get the audience back on board with their act. Or, they didn't have the skill, that is the ability to actually ride the wave of conversation with the audience, either because they didn't listen, or because they couldn't respond properly.

If you've ever been on a cold call or any sales conversation that has derailed you'll notice that it's due to the same reasons: because you either didn't have the tools or you didn't have the skills. Now, the skills can be learned, the tools can be created, but you must have a foundation of good listening in order to know either of those things. The foundation for all good sales comes from good listening skills.

In any sales conversation you're having you need to actually display a lot of value, and value is displayed firstly through good listening skills. So, if you're calling someone up on the phone and they answer, they say, "It's a bad time." The *wrong* thing to do is to continue talking. Many sales & prospecting programs tell you to continue talking. They say you should go through your script, you should just steamroll and continue speaking. If they hang up on you, that's okay.

That's not the kind of sales we're talking about here; we're talking about how to connect with high value people. If they say they're too busy to speak, then they're too busy to speak. You don't want to destroy the rapport you're trying to create with someone before creating it by not listening to them. High-value people have only time in their life for others who can add value to their lives by understanding them and listening to them. A good way to get yourself taken out of consideration is by displaying that you don't know how to listen, and you're not going to hear anything they have to say.

Basically, when you're not listening, you're telling the person you're interacting with that the things they're telling you aren't important or valuable. Anyone who has any self-worth is going to have no time for anyone who communicates those things.

The good news, though, is that, good listening skills can be learned. Here are some quick tactics: First, practice the mirroring technique. Get on the phone and match your prospects tone. You want to match them but be slightly more positive, you're aiming to resonate. You're aiming not to outdo them, but you want to slightly pump their state by sounding just a little more positive. If you're practicing being in a good state and organizing your outreach, you should already sound this way, but *listen* to your prospect and try and match their tone. You don't want to go in too enthusiastic because that'll break rapport and will seem inauthentic. So, use the mirroring technique to reflect back tone in a conversation, try it out with people in your life and you'll get good at it quickly.

Good stand-up comedians and improvisers do this. They get on stage and respond to the real essence of the audience and meet the audience where it's at, not where the comedian is. Again, if sales and comedy are both about leadership, then pay attention to what good leaders do. They don't ignore the state of the people they're trying to lead, but they don't wallow in it either. Good leaders start where the people they want to lead are, and then *lead them somewhere else*.

If you get on the phone, and you speak with someone and they say, "Oh, my day is terrible." You say, "Wow! Sounds bad. Sounds like I caught you in a bad time." Respond authentically, this communicates that you are actually listening to what they're saying. Probably, a lot of sales coaches who would say something like, "Don't do that. Be positive. Move through it, don't acknowledge it. Go through the script. Steamroll!" But if you do this, you're actually going to alienate your prospect. Simply acknowledging it by saying "Oh, sounds like you're having a hard day," is leaps and bounds more successful than steamrolling. Remember, just because it's a cold call doesn't mean it has to be a sales conversation, because it's not. It's actually a human conversation. Every conversation you have is at the first level a human conversation.

Comedians can fail by blowing themselves out of rapport with an audience because they'll get in front of an audience and immediately begin rolling through their material, telling their jokes, without addressing how an audience is. If another comedian just got offstage and made it very awkward for one reason or another then it doesn't make any sense to get on stage and not acknowledge the awkwardness. Just mentioning the strange atmosphere is actually practicing good listening. If you get on stage and say something like, "Wow, it's weird in this room right now, right?"

You and the audience are on the same page. Just like that, the same thing is true in a cold call. By acknowledging it, you're actually going to resonate with your audience. That type of authenticity and honesty builds rapport. And that's a rapport that you can use to lead your audience somewhere else.

Laughter comes from an audience being pleasantly rather than painfully surprised. It's actually evolutionary; it's based in our genes. And expressing that laugh is an indication that they've followed the comedian to where he led them. On a cold call you want to do something similar. If you can get someone to laugh at you or if you can get someone to resonate with you if you reflect what you heard from them in that moment, "Wow, sounds like you're having a hard day." They'll probably respond positively, "Oh, man. Totally is!" Bang! You've got them hooked.

Grant Cardone, the famous sales guru (I have no idea what else to call him) says something similar. He says that if you're on a call, someone is getting sold: either you're sold that you can't get a meeting and you're giving up, or they're sold that you two should continue talking. If you're trying to sell them on the idea that you two should continue talking, a good way to do that is by listening and by reflecting it back to them.

Working Through Bits

So, here's where we get to some of the meat of the book! The difference between scripts and bits.

Scripts, as I've stated before, are straightforward. They're written out. They go from one line to another. They have a definite order; you have to go through them from one beat to another, from point A to point B, all the way to point Z. While you go through the script, the intention is to take a prospect with you by hitting all the points. This sometimes leads to the illusion that the *script* is the magical thing; that just by getting the words out, it'll work and you'll make sales.

If you have ever used scripts in your own job position then you know that they don't work—that's just the truth, they don't really work. Scripts rarely work. You have to improvise, go off-script, speak extemporaneously. Most of the time when you're on-script it feels impersonal, it feels like you don't have control, because you don't, the script does. Speaking the words of the script feels strange for you, and it feels strange for the prospect to listen to. The truth is this: if you don't resonate with any of this then you're probably a sociopath, don't care about what prospects think or feel, and you should return this book for a full refund. Nothing I can say will help you, and God have mercy on your family, friends and colleagues.

Bits, however, are different. Bits are short talk tracks. Bits are able to be dropped at any point in a conversation that you feel they'll resonate with your prospect and bring them from point A to point B. Bits create micro changes in conversation. But all those small changes, like telling many jokes, add up to a prospect buying into what you're selling.

I want you to think about bits like jokes, like anecdotes or like short stories, things that you, if you were at a cocktail party would use to entertain an audience briefly and go from a point A to point B. Bits are used to build rapport, to take someone from one place to another; you have a lot of them that you already use in your daily life. The truth is that you have to practice them in the same way that a stand-up comedian practices their jokes.

Bits make you more flexible to be yourself, and that's important because you're selling *yourself*. The comedian sells themselves on stage; the salesperson and sales development rep sells themselves in conversation over the phone. Bits leave gaps in conversation that let you put your own charisma and your own personality into to bring the conversation to a new place.

Bits have three parts: a set-up, some value, and a question. So, stand-up comedy is like this—jokes have a setup and a punch line.

Jokes set-up something very quickly with some emotion, some loaded imagery, and then they have a punch line that completes that feeling. That's a quick and dirty way of describing them, but that's basically the way that they work. Look up all jokes, they all work like this. "Why did the chicken cross the road? To get to the other side." That's the setup, that's the punch line.

Bits are similar to jokes. The set-up to a bit can be something like "I noticed you have a loyalty program," that opens something very quickly; we're talking about your loyalty program, your loyalty program is publicly available and I noticed it. The value might be something like, "My company has helped clients that look a lot like you improve their loyalty program by 10x." And the question is the punchline: "Is there someone on your team I can connect with about it?" That's a bit; that's something you can practice over and over. You might not say that in the same way to everyone, but you're going to say it *like that* to someone.

As you're going to go from person to person you can modify the bit and continue to drop it into cold calls, "I notice you have a loyalty program." "Hey, I signed up for your loyalty program." "Look, I know your loyalty program is online. I found this article that was written about it." "Actually, I just got some points on your loyalty program but we helped another company improve 10x—this result, and I'm looking to connect with the person who is responsible, is that you?"

Or, you could say something more specific: "I'm looking to connect with Marsha Fowler, she looks like from my research the person to speak with about the loyalty program. Is that correct?" These are all bits. You can you can tailor them to your audience and make them more relevant or less relevant; it's really a structure in the same way that jokes have a structure, set-up, and punchline. You can write out the bits and modify on-the-fly to be more relevant to your audience.

You'll also notice that bits are simple and spartan. The audience's brain can't handle too much information. You don't want to go into too much detail. You don't want to say, "Hey, I looked at your loyalty program—your point based loyalty program—what my company offers is a series of leverages that maximize the synergy between two different customer touchpoints in your program." Those are all big words. They're too much for the brain of your audience. Will I ever have said that in front of an audience like a joke? The joke would be that I sound like an idiot.

Information must be delivered slowly enough for your audience to get it. Contrast this with how many cold-callers speak very quickly when their prospect picks up. Typically, they speak in big words, they speak in vague words; they require a lot of energy from the prospect to actually work through their pitch. If you look at the way most comedians deliver material, it's very sparse. Many successful comedians actually go through every single word in their jokes to see if they can cut down the number of syllables needed in the joke. If they can use shorter, smaller, easier to understand words in the place of larger, more encumbering, more vague words, they're going to err on the side of a simpler words.

Again, you want to make things simple, because your prospects brain is going to feel less threatened by large words that require them to spend mental energy figuring out what you're saying to them, especially while you're interrupting their day. So, refine your bits; take your talk tracks from your script and break them into their smallest component parts, then memorize those, internalize them.

To be clear, the sales situation is actually different when you already have your audience's attention. So, if you're in a meeting and someone is giving you a lot of attention to understand your product, to understand your service, and you have their attention free from distractions, speaking quickly and moving through ideas at a fast clip actually does make sense if there's a lot to move through.

Assignment: Bits vs Scripts

Here's your assignment for this section. If you do it, it will help your sales game go to the next level in terms of your ability to close cold calls into meetings, and help progress meetings that you have from one stage to another in your sales process.

Basically, this is what you want to do: Write down your pitches. Take your talk tracks and write them down *verbatim* – either longhand, or type them up on a computer. Write them all the way out in the way you would say it, word for word. Say it out loud, as you write it down. Do you really have to say it out loud and write it down verbatim? Yes.

Now, take a moment and go through it word by word. As you go through your pitch, eliminate words, and even syllables that do not need to be there. Replace complicated words with simple ones, aim for an elementary-school comprehension level.

So, if you have a very wordy, word heavy pitch with three, four, even five syllable words, break the pitch down into simpler words. A pitch that might start out by saying, "We leverage our customers efficiencies in order to, blah blah blah," turns into "We find ways customers can XYZ." That's it. It doesn't have to be wordy, it has to be simple and easy to understand. Eliminate big words, eliminate syllables that don't need to be there.

Finally, craft responses to the way you think your audience might react to you. Come up with a comeback for a yes, a no, or a maybe. This is actually something comedians do often. Comedians come up with bits, they develop material, then they *anticipate* how an audience might respond and they write different talk tracks and jokes for each potential response. You can do the same thing with your pitches and bits. Think about how someone might respond if they push back, if they say let's go ahead. Take a moment to have a sense for where the conversation is going to go after you deliver your simple pitch. It doesn't have to be a full sales process, don't map out the entire conversation like a programmer, but have a sense for how your audience may respond and what you would say to them in that situation.

YOUR #1 JOB

I want you to think about something. I want you to think about the world your prospect lives in. I want you to think about their day-to-day.

You make calls to people – maybe hundreds of people, maybe thousands of people. Maybe you make 100, 200, 300 calls a day. Maybe you only make a few. But, when you make calls to people, what you're trying to do is impose *your* agenda on *them*. You have an agenda. You have something you want *them* to do. You're trying to gain some compliance from them.

But, think about what their day-to-day is like. In the B2B sales environment your normal prospect is probably receiving dozens, if not hundreds of calls every day, week-over-week from people who want their attention. They see the good, they see the bad, they see the ugly.

Most of the sales development people who reach out to the same prospects you're trying to talk to don't know much about those prospects. Most salespeople don't know much about the prospects they're dialing. They don't know about the prospect's world, they don't know about the things the prospect does, they don't know about the prospect personally, and they don't even know about the prospect's job, just the prospect's title. These salespeople are just trying to impose *their* agenda on *your* prospect. And honestly, those salespeople don't care to know much.

They have too many things going on. Those salespeople are reaching out, calling day-in and day-out trying to make something happen for themselves.

Your prospect has developed a series of defenses to prevent their time from being wasted by those lame salespeople, and also to guard their emotions. It hurts to say no. It hurts to have someone who wants you to do something for them and you tell them no. Basically, these salespeople are not adding any value to the prospect's life. That's the truth. They're salespeople who are reaching out, trying to get something, and *taking value*. They're constantly trying to get. They're not really trying to give. They may have even convinced themselves that they're trying to give. But they're not. They're trying to take.

So, your prospect has learned to listen to a handful of ques to tell if this stranger calling is worth any time; tone, the way the person is speaking to them on the phone, questions the salesperson asks, all of these things. Your prospect has learned to assess very quickly what to say no to and how to shut a cold caller down.

So how can you get beyond these defenses? Ask yourself this question: "How can I be the type of person that my prospect wants to speak with?"

How do you bypass their defenses? Well, it's really simple. Your number one job, the first thing you have to do when reaching out to prospects by cold calling is *be different* from every other person who's trying to reach out to them. That's it! All you have to do is be different.

Your number one job is to look different to your prospects.

In comedy, this is very similar. There's an unwritten rule in stand-up called, "Don't be the last guy on stage." It means what it says: you do not want to be the same as the last comedian who just got offstage. If that guy was good, then you don't want to be him because you're going to look worse. If he was bad, then you don't want to be him because the audience is going to think you suck from the beginning.

In a cold calling situation, you have no idea who the last guy was. Your prospect gets hit up hundreds of times a day. But, you can ask yourself a few questions: what do we know about normal sales reps? What stereotypes do we know about normal salespeople who prospect? 1. They're pushy. 2. They have not done any research. 3. They just keep talking. 4. They're nervous. 5. They don't listen.

Now, ask yourself this question: Who are the people in your life who are worth talking to? Who adds value to your life? Why? Who are the people who if you started speaking with them you would want to keep talking with them? What do they do? Probably, their number one quality is that they're good listeners. Probably, they know something about your world. So how do you display these things? You have to research. You have to be positive and you have actual have value to offer. So be opposite of how all the rest of the salespeople are.

If we just convert the equation of what makes a bad salesperson to its opposite, the direction on how to behave is pretty clear: 1. Be patient. 2. Know things about your prospects world and why what you have to offer could be valuable to them. 3. Listen! And respond by showing that you've heard your prospect. Repeat what you've heard back to them. Show that what they've said to you actually affects and changes the way you are behaving. 4. Remain calm when they have an emotional response.

Not every prospect you catch is going to be having the best day of their life. Most often, they'll probably be frustrated that someone they don't know caught them on the phone and sounds a lot like a hundred other people who have wasted their time in the past. Be patient with them. Instead of reacting, listen to what they have to say, maybe try to make a very quick case for why you're different. "Hey, I'm sorry didn't mean to derail your day. You know what, I'd like to forward you some info. Apologies again!" Very few people have said that *authentically* to them. You can follow up politely and persistently later and *they will remember you.*

Finally, always be honest and authentic. Make a commitment to yourself. Make a commitment to your job that you're going to develop all of your conversations with honesty and authenticity. If you are sorry, say you're sorry. If you're frustrated, say "Hey, you know what, I've been trying to reach out to you for six months and I've been calling you twice a week. I get the feeling you're avoiding my calls and you don't want to talk. But it's okay for you to say 'no' to me. Can you just say that in this moment?" A lot of so-called sales gurus and coaches are going to tell you never to say those words. But if you express them, they might resonate with your prospect. Sure, they could say you "no". They could say, "Hey, go away. I don't want to talk to you." But at least you got it from the horse's mouth, and maybe it's actually going to cause them to open up and listen to what you have to say.

This comes down ethos. Remember that from earlier? You have to be *the kind of person* someone wants to talk to. Comedy, as Seinfeld once said, is all about style. So is early pipelines sales. Who you are, how you come off, is your style. The best style to have is a straightforward, solid style on the phone. Practice good character, be a value add. If you can get a prospect to say, "Man, that call what that salesperson actually went great." Or, "Man, the call with that salesperson was really actually wonderful." Then you're world-class, because nobody but nobody is able to deliver that kind of value.

Aim to be that kind of person on the phone with every call that you have. If you make that your goal and you pursue it in a way that is efficient and organized, you will be different from everyone else, and complete your number one job. Complete that number one job and you'll be without a doubt one of the best sales people, cold callers, and relationship builders in the world.

Things to Show Quickly

The first 10 seconds of a cold call is a very, very special time. It's fraught with lots of tension, emotion, doubt, confusion. Frankly, there's very little as exciting and dramatic than hearing a prospect pick up. It could lead to yet another hang up for you, or the beginning of a multi-million dollar relationship.

In the first 10 to 20 seconds of a call, you have the opportunity to display to the prospect you could be a very high value person. You have to power to cause the prospect to think "Oh! This is somebody I want to listen to."

The first thing to show is that you've done the research. If you show that you actually know something about their world this will really perk their ears up. Show that you know who they are, look them up on Google, on LinkedIn, and repeat back to them exactly who they are. That's why it's good to say, "Hey, I'm reaching out to you because from my research it looked like you handle the email service program at XYZ Corp, is that true?" And they're probably going to respond, "Yeah, that's me," or "No, that's someone else," or "How'd you get this number!?" If you get a referral to someone else, you should lead with that. "Hey, I was just talking to Nancy Pickard in the loyalty department, she said you were the person to speak with who best understands the email program, is that correct?"

Getting a referral, and mentioning it to the prospect displays a lot of high value "Hey, I've actually been around your company and I know who you are, I've done the research, and you're the person I've been told to speak with." It's different than someone calling and going, "Hi, I'm calling to talk about your XYZ program." Or, "Hi, I'm just trying to call and talk about email solutions" All of that is very low value. Display that you've done research very quickly, the more specific and timely the research, the better.

Try to find something interesting in the marketplace to say, like a relevant news article or video from a conference, let your prospect know very succinctly and specifically right at the beginning of your call. "Hey, I know from research that you guys are currently using a Tact2 servicing protocol on your email program, is that true? I've read an article about problems with those; it looks like you could be falling prey to the same thing that three or four other companies I've spoken to this week have been falling prey to. Can I show you what I showed them?" That's very specific, but it displays that you know a lot and you could have a lot of value to offer. Obviously, your pitch is going to sound a bit different, but try to make it as specific as you can.

If you use a specific example that they aren't aware of and they say "No I didn't, I wasn't; wait, hold on a second, there could be a problem with my email program?" That's a strong indication you've added value and it triggers something in their brain that says to them "This person knows what they're talking about. This person has some information that's relevant to my world and I should probably listen to them."

It's so important to show that you know what their business is that you can begin to understand where so many cold calls go wrong. Salespeople who call and ask an open-ended question, especially right at the beginning, are asking the *prospect* to do their job for them. Don't do this. Instead, do the work and then display you've done it.

At the same time as you're displaying some knowledge of their world, you also want to avoid trying to show that you know more about their world than *they do*. Stay humble. You might know one or two things more than they know about their world, but generally, they have authority. For example, let's say you call a prospect about their email program, about their technology program, about their hiring practices, about whatever you want to speak with them about. You might know more about this *exact* part of their business, but they know more about their business in general.

To communicate your exploratory demeanor, you want to use phrases that indicate that you don't know *for certain* that you have a solution for them, but there's a *possibility* of value that's worth further investigation. What you're looking to do is try to *invite them* into a discussion on whether or not what you're calling about is relevant to them and if and how much value it can have. Invite them to be curious. Invite them to collaborate in the investigation.

You want to use phrases here to inspire curiosity but *not* ultimate confidence yet. Other coaches and sales programs are going to tell you not to use phrases like "I don't know for sure," but that's actually a good thing to lead off with in a call. "Look, I don't assume to know. I'm just trying to see if there's value here." "Potentially," or "Maybe," those are phrases that you want to use.

Too much certainty is threatening to a prospect who doesn't know you yet. It feels sharp, uncomfortable, and invites interrogative questions back such as "How do you know? What makes you think you know anything about my business?" But more than anything else, unbridled confidence from a salesperson sets off alarms to the prospect that dealing with this salesperson is going to be *work*. Instead, use your language to *invite them* to collaborate with you to see if you have value to offer them.

Use phrases to indicate value like "We've worked with people who look a lot like you and I'd like to see if there's an opportunity to work with you in the same way to provide you with similar value." Almost no other sales literature is going to tell you to say phrases like that. Instead, most sales books will say things like, "I'm certain. I know this. You're going to see the value, it's going to be amazing." But this leaves no room for your prospect to explore with you whether or not there's a fit.

So, what I would say to bring it all together is something like this, just to use my last company as an example:

Me: "Hi, my name is Brendon. I'm calling from Citron Corp. I just was looking to speak with you Brian, because from my research, it looked like you're the person who handles the mobile loyalty program at XYZ Corp, is that correct?"

Brian: "Yes, no, maybe, I'm not sure." (Whatever they come back with)

Me: "Oh, okay, cool. I've got a couple of other references including the VP of Sales, David Kirby's office told me that you were the person to speak with. Well, here's what I'm looking to call about. I know that XYZ Corp has a loyalty program, but I could see that you're currently not leveraging mobile marketing, which I know is a big opportunity for a company like yours because we just worked with ABC Corp, and we improved their loyalty program value by 10x just by adding the ability to send text messages instead of only emails." -Pause-

Brian: (Catching up in his brain) "Okay?"

Me: "So what's interesting is that the lift for ABC, quarter-over-quarter, was about 15 dollars per subscriber which ultimately led to a program that was valued at over 10 million dollars. So, I just wanted to see – and I'm not really sure, but I wanted to see if you would be open to setting some time just to talk a little bit further because it looks like this could be something XYZ Corp could do too. Would you be open to setting some time?"

This kind of pitch actually works really well to set meetings. Quickly, I showed Brian that I knew something about what his business does, what he does and who he is, then moved to indicating value using a couple of easy to understand data points, then invited him to explore whether or not there's value for him with me. I did this in only about 200 words, and arguably could've used even less. I challenge you to use the above pitch and cut it down to 175 words.

The final thing to show for sure in the first few seconds of the phone call is that you're actually listening to your prospect. If somebody says this isn't the time to talk, take it. Take the loss, call back later. "Got it, what would be a good time to call back?" Just ask that question back. "Okay, sorry, I didn't mean to interrupt. What would be a good time? Do you mind if I send you an invite just to hold the timeslot?"

Even though your prospect doesn't know who you are and you've never spoken before you'll be surprised how often you can set an appointment this way because most people are going to be polite. If they really don't want to talk and they say, "Look, I don't know who you are. So just please send me something." Take them at their word. "Okay, sure, absolutely. I'll send you an email. Sorry for taking up too much of your time. It sounds like you're busy." Then remind them in the subject line, "Sorry for interrupting you."

There's a lot of sales coaches who will tell you not to apologize for interrupting, or not to remind prospects that you bothered them. Here's the thing, that was such a small blip on their radar, but they will remember who you are. They're going to go, "Oh, that's that guy who actually listened to me." Plus, if you have something compelling to say to them in that email, they will open it up and take a look. And if they won't, it doesn't matter. You're going to follow-up and call them anyway.

So, show that you're actually listening and don't get on your prospect's bad side. Why is it important? Because nobody does it. Again, just like in improv comedy, you don't want to dismiss. don't say "No". Use a "yes, and." As a great example of this, I once sent an email to an executive at a large gym chain across America. I said in the email "Can I buy you a cup of coffee?" And she emailed back, "No." Just "N-O," no. Within moments of receiving it I replied and said, "Okay. Protein shake, Moscow Mule?" The next email I got back was "Hahahahaha, that's really funny. I checked out your website, here's why I think we can't work together. Maybe follow up in a few months, we'll have a conversation. I understand what you do but right now, I'm busy and also I don't think this is a good fit for these reasons."

I still got a "no" or at least a "not right now," but she actually put some effort into telling me why it wouldn't work out together. But why did that work? It's because I didn't refuse the no; I took it and just twisted it around. That's what I want you to do. Show that you're listening and take the conversation to whatever place you want to get to. Don't just plow through it. Don't say, "Listen, you don't know because I blah, blah, blah."

Have a sense of humor. Be slightly detached from what's happening and if you show a prospect you're slightly detached early in the call, early in the conversation, by using words like "maybe," or "potentially," etc. They're going to feel the lack of emotional tension and they'll feel comfortable with you on the phone. They'll feel comfortable answering your questions because they feel that you won't make it uncomfortable for them if you don't like their answers.

This also works, by the way, because they're probably not listening to you. They're probably thinking "Who is this person? I got a lot of things going on." If you twist something they say around and actually reiterate it to them, repeating back to them what they just said in a way that sounds like you registered it, they're actually going to be surprised, because until that point they're probably not *really* listening to you. Getting feedback on something they just said snaps their brain into paying attention.

So if, as another example, I said to someone once, "Do you know who handles your email program?" And they said, "No". And I said with a laugh "Okay, your title is email manager. So it sounds like you should know that kind of thing." And they laughed, and admitted that they did, and that they were the person.

Understand, this is all about frame control, and frame control at this level is about demeanor, tone, and about your ability to stay grounded. The person who stays grounded and who can be vulnerable and honest is the higher value person in the conversation. I've mentioned it before and it's worth mentioning again: be honest, be knowledgeable that you know who they are, be a good listener, be open and willing to explore with them. If you trigger these things early in the call, they'll not only take your call but will genuinely pay attention. And if they don't want to, they'll give you real reasons why they don't.

Authenticity

We've talked about bits, we've talked about trying to gain compliance, and displaying that you have knowledge of the prospect's world, but here's the thing, you can show very quickly that you're actually a low-value person by being inauthentic. Prospects have a very good barometer on whether or not someone is being completely honest with them, and if they smell dishonestly, inauthenticity, it'll throw them off and you'll get hung up on.

If you are dishonest, or if you say something you think is honest but you don't actually know if it's true or not, your prospect is going to tell very quickly. Now, comedians know this because if you get on stage and say something you're not 100% committed to, and don't really believe in, the crowd's going to feel it. The crowd will actually turn against you. They're not going to believe what you say, and they're not going to get on board with you. They won't trust you when you try to lead them. Remember, comedy is evolutionarily rooted in something that was surprising, but actually surprising in a good way rather than a scary way, they're not going to want to *follow* you because they know that this surprise could be bad and can't trust you.

Leadership, sales, and comedy are all built on gaining the trust of an audience and the fastest way to lose trust is by being dishonest, inauthentic, or outright lying. Don't do these things, ever. Everyone knows the stereotype of the lying, say-anything-to-get-the-sale salesman. Don't be him. His life is horrible in and out of the office. His wife will leave him and take the kids.

Comedians develop a feel for the way the crowd follows them, and they know that they have to be honest with the crowd. If a comedian is fake with the crowd, if they are inauthentic it scares a crowd away from following them. They have no ethos, no character. Nobody wants to follow someone with no character.

When you're being honest, you are actually also being vulnerable. When you're speaking the truth on the call, about the prospect, about the opportunity, about what you think the opportunity for the prospect might be, even if you're being 100% honest, somebody could really turn away from you because you might say, "Look, I don't know if this is a real opportunity or not." Someone could say, "Well then, why am I wasting my time?" And hang up on you. "Why are you calling me?" But, the high-value people who you're probably trying to connect with are likely not going to behave that way. Instead, they'll likely recognize your character and respect it.

So, if you say something like, "Look, I don't know if this is going to be a true opportunity." And someone says to you, "Well then, I suggest you do some research and figure out if it could be and where it could be and get back to me." They *just* told you how to get a meeting with them. So you know that you need to leave, go do more research, come back with a very convincing value prop tailored just to them, and then get that meeting because they told you exactly how to get it. And notice, they engaged with you. They gave you a real answer. That's not a "no." That's not a "I'm not going to meet with you." That's a "Here's how you get a meeting with me." So you need to understand that their honesty back to you is a reflection of your honesty to them. That's basically what it's about.

Some other things that you can say that are honest are "I don't know." This is really good to get out early in a conversation. If someone says to you, "So, how could this exactly help me?" Say, "Look, I know that what we've done for people in the past who look like you has been very helpful to them. But I can't tell you right now in this early phone call, *exactly* how it's going to help you. That's going to require some more conversation, but what I'd like to do is invite you into that conversation to see if it could be a fit. Does that make sense?" Your prospect, if they're a reasonable person, will probably say, "Yeah, actually that does kind of make sense. You're right, it's a technical answer." Or, "No, I don't have time for this. I have a lot of competing priorities." To which, in turn, you can say, "Fair enough, is 20 minutes too much time? How about 15? We can go from there."

When you're honest, and you listen to prospects, they actually give you the keys to how to get a meeting with them. If you just listen to what they're saying, by being honest and vulnerable, and accept being vulnerable is a necessity to being honest, then your vulnerability and honest will inspire their vulnerability and honesty. It's called the Law of Reciprocity. It was discovered by a guy named Robert Cialdini and it's actually hardwired into the human brain. For them to open up a bit they need for you to open up a bit first. And if you're a high-value person who's grounded, you're going to be willing to go ahead and do that.

If a prospect says to you, "Listen, you seem very convinced, but I have no idea how this is going to help me, do you?" You can always say "I don't," and then start laughing. That laughing, that admission of "Oh boy, this is just too much." That laughter is actually going to cause relief on their end. No one can laugh when things are too tense. No one can laugh when there's too much skin in the game. If you start laughing, you're going to show that you don't have a lot of skin in this game. You're communicating that although you're trying to get a meeting, it's not that big of a deal, you're trying to get a meeting with 100 other people too. So if you say no, it's really not that big of a deal. Remember, you have 99 more chances. You're making calls in a good mood, you're a fun person, and if the prospect meets with you, the two of you are going to have fun (hopefully you're already having fun on that cold call). Also, actually, that conversation could be worth 10 million dollars to them. This kind of carefree but invested attitude is actually going to really inspire their trust in you, because you were willing to be vulnerable and that's what trust is actually based on. That's what you're trying to do in early pipeline sales, develop rapport and then inspire trust. You can't have trust without rapport, for sure.

The reason this is important both in sales and comedy is that audiences have to trust you. The only way to trust you is by seeing your vulnerabilities; just as you have to trust them by seeing theirs. You're aware that you could hurt them, waste their time or pressure them uncomfortably. You could draw them into something they don't want to talk about, you could put them in an uncomfortable situation, you could be a pushy bad salesperson, but your vulnerability is the thing that reassures them that that is not going to happen.

The next time you're on a call and you are stuck, say something like this, "Yeah, I don't know where to go from here. Where do you think we should go from here?" You'll be surprised how your prospect will sometimes open up and begin to collaborate with you right there on the call. If you genuinely don't know where to go, but it feels like there could be some interest between the two of you, just say "I don't really know where to go from here, where do you think we should go from here?" A very successful salesman at an office I worked at used to say that all the time. "How do we develop this from here?" is what he would say. Then, like a miracle, the prospect would lay out answers for him. It was really surprising to me as a young salesman. Somehow, as soon as he'd gained a bit of rapport and they'd seen value, he'd gotten them inside the circle and now all of us were on the same team.

So, again, if you lose someone from being vulnerable and honest on a call, if somebody says, "Listen, I need a strong reason, I need you to know that this isn't something that can come to my attention unless my CEO says so," they're actually giving you the keys to how to get a meeting with them. Keep that in mind.

Things to Show Very Quickly Assignment

Here's your assignment for this section: Sit down and think about the last few times you've heard someone say something like the previous exchange but you took their response as a "No." Write down a couple of these things that you could've said.

Take a moment, and on a piece of paper, write down a couple of things that you've heard and taken as a no. Next, write down how you could work around what they said. Responses you've received like, "Yeah, no. We don't evaluate partners who haven't been working with us for a couple of years. We don't, we actually don't listen to anyone new who hasn't come through a referral network. Well I don't do anything that CEO doesn't tell me to do," are actually solutions in disguise. They're a bread-crumb trail that leads in the direction of eventually doing business.

DISMISSALS

So, the bane of every sales development rep's life... dismissals.

Dismissals are a little different from objections. In most sales theory, you're going to hear a lot about handling objections. I don't want to deal with objection handling directly here, there's a lot of resources on dealing with objections that you can check out online. There's really a lot that has already been said about it. The problem with "objection handling" is that objections actually rarely come up in cold calls. However, there is a type of objection that you regularly get that I call a "dismissal." This is when a prospect isn't saying "no" to working with you, they're saying "no" to talking with you right at that moment.

A lot of sales literature on objections handling talks about overcoming objections. Most objections handling focuses on giving *reasons* for why the objection doesn't interrupt working together. So, a prospect saying something like "Oh, we're already working with someone." Might elicit a response like "Oh! No worries, most of the people we speak with already have one partner, but after hearing the differences we provide most people end up switching to our services."

However, when you're getting dismissed, none of that crap will work. Nobody who is dismissing you wants to hear that stuff. They're not even in a position to hear it. Traditional sales books might say "Hey, overcome their unwillingness to listen to you with old-school persistence and tenacity." Eh, maybe. Most of the time, in a phone call, steamrolling like that is really bad for developing a relationship. And yeah, you can push through a dismissal, but, if you're dealing with a high value person, they're probably going to think "This salesperson is not listening to me, they're an idiot." And they'll just hang up the phone. If you did that to me, I wouldn't listen either.

When you get a dismissal, it's the prospect saying "no" to having a conversation with you *right then*. They're not saying no to anything that has any real logic to it. Early in a phone call, a prospect telling you that they're working with someone already doesn't really make any sense because you're not even talking with them about seriously working together yet.

Let's imagine that you have a cell phone and someone tries to sell you another phone. You might say "You know what, no thanks, I've already got a phone." But if somebody came along with a phone that was a hundred times better for one fifth of the price of your phone, and they say, "Literally this phone will change your tires for you, it'll do your taxes, you can talk into it, it'll find you a girlfriend or a boyfriend; it *actually* does do all of these things! I can demonstrate it and actually it only costs $200."

In this case, you would be an idiot not to take that deal. If such a thing existed, your excuse that you already had a phone would not be a real objection because it's not addressing any of the logical components the salesman is putting forward. Yeah, you already have a phone, but we're not talking about just a phone anymore. We're talking about something that makes phone calls *in addition* to solving all of your life's problems.

In this case, if you said "I already have a phone," it'd be out of refusing to have a conversation, not about *the phone*. It'd be an *unqualified* "no." Unless you're a total dweeb and want to keep your dumb phone that doesn't change your tires. Who knows, some people still like their old Nokia brick phones.

When you understand where dismissals come from you'll see why prospects do so many illogical and ridiculous things on cold calls. Once I called and prospect and said "I want to talk about your email program." And they said, "We already have a partner." And I responded, "Oh, that's interesting. I did my research, I didn't see an email partner." And they said "Oh, actually we don't have a partner." Well why the hell didn't they say they had a partner at first!? It's because they were saying "no" to me in the moment. Saying "no" to a conversation, and "partner" was the first thing their brain grabbed on to.

So a dismissal is just that. It's refusing to talk to you, right then, at *that* moment. It's refusing the conversation. It's refusing someone bothering them. It's refusing the phone call that came in at 10:17 when they have to finish writing emails.

The dismissal itself is not logical. There's no logical component to it. If you try to deal with the dismissal logically then you're actually failing to understand what's really happening. So, that's what you want to think about when it comes to dismissals. If you call someone and they say "I'm heading into a meeting," no one answers a phone call when they're heading into a meeting, that's ridiculous.

So, how do you get over this dismissal? It's pretty simple. Stay calm, and don't really acknowledge it. So, if somebody says "I'm heading into a meeting," simply say "Oh, man! You sound busy," and then go into your pitch really quickly. "Well, it sounds busy, I'll be very quick. Here's what I'm calling about." Finish your pitch.

If they say "We already work with a partner." You say "Oh, wow! That's crazy. A lot of people work with a lot of people, I guess. Anyway, I'm calling to talk about blah, blah, blah, blah, blah."

Now, this might sound counterintuitive because I've already said you should listen. What I was talking about when I said "listening" before is actually *do* listen to what your prospect says, but recognize the fact that what you're listening for is a *real* "no" or a *real* "not now." If they're not hearing you yet, they're not listening to you yet.

Most of the time, prospects don't even understand what you're talking about in the first moments of a cold call. Their brain is thinking a lot, two or three things at once maybe; they answered the phone call, maybe they don't have enough time to actually focus on the logical components of the message you're pitching them. In this case, you can respond by being aloof. "Oh, we already have a partner," they might say. You can respond with "That's fine, we'll be your better partner. Maybe you can be polyamorous." I would say that to someone on the phone, they'll probably laugh! Maybe they won't even know what the word polyamorous means. You could follow up with "Date around! Try a couple of email service providers, you know." That kind of stuff is light-hearted, and it acknowledges what they said, but it doesn't treat it like it's a real thing, which it isn't most of the time.

Keep a positive and detached attitude, and demeanor and you'll overcome all dismissals. Now at some point, your prospect might say "You know what, we don't have an opportunity." Listen to what they say. Those real reasons are actually an objection. So if they say, "You know what, we're actually in a three-year contract with a partner. It would cost us over a $100,000 to get out. We don't have the budget or time for it right now." That's a *real* objection. That's something that you can deal with. You have to *deal* with that objection by saying something like "Well maybe, if there was a way that we could help you do this for free, or we can enable with our team, your report over so that it wouldn't be so expensive, and we would pay for your contract breaking fee if you were to sign with us, would that be something that would maybe be intriguing to you to move forward together?" That's an objection; that's you removing the objection.

I always say to take the third "no" a prospect gives. So if somebody dismisses me with "Oh, I'm heading into a meeting." And I say "Oh, this will only take a second. I just want to talk to you." Then they say "You know what, I actually really don't have time right now." I would say, "Okay, great. I'll make it super short. I'm just trying to..." And finally, they interrupt with "Actually you know what, I can't talk right now." I would respond with "kay, my bad. Take it easy, didn't mean to interrupt. I'll send you an email, we'll talk later." That's it. Take the third no.

If you can't get anything from a prospect and you're getting hung up on, but you haven't gotten a qualified "no" yet, continue to prospect. A qualified "no" is a "no" with an explanation. So if you get a "no" and get hung up on, ask yourself these questions: Have I been heard? Does this prospect know what they're saying no to? If they don't know what they're saying no to, then you haven't been heard and that's not a qualified no. *Always* take a qualified no.

As a salesperson, it's your job to provide value to your prospect even if your prospect isn't aware and isn't listening to you. You have to overcome those things. It's hard, but that is actually the job. There's a lot of prospects that I've dealt with and this has happened before, who've said, "You know, we're already working with partner and we're completely satisfied." And I said, "Wow, that's cool. Are you having any trouble with your partner?" And they immediately respond with "You know what, actually we are. Our current partner actually is awful!"

Why would they do that? It's because they weren't actually listening or considering anything I was saying. All it took was one little snag, one little poke. This is why there is no silver bullet for overcoming a dismissal, for getting a prospect to pay attention. So the "I'm going to a meeting, can I call you later?" response can be met with "Sure, what time would be better?" Then *actually* calling them back at that time. Better yet, send them an email invite for that time. Take them at their word. "Can I forward to you a quick link to schedule a good time to call back?"

I once said to a prospect "I'm looking for the person who handles the email program," and they said "You know, I don't know who that person is." And I quickly shot back, "Oh, is it your first day? How's it going? Things working out?" I said it in such a way that it wasn't condescending, it was just funny. The prospect laughed and said "Look, I don't really know. That person is in a different department. Go check with this person." They gave me a name and I followed up.

Take prospect's at their word. Overcome with an honest question "If you were me where would you go from here?" Keep the aloof attitude, the fun, the positivity. Think of something in the moment and just go with it. Once you create that fun, aloof attitude you'll actually find yourself very easily overcoming dismissals. Get laughs from prospects and you'll be referred to the right people. You'll get real consideration because you snap their brain out of autopilot.

Here's as close to a silver-bullet as you can get: If your prospect is really pushing back on you a couple of times and dismissing you hard, you can always just laugh and say "Man, you do not want to talk to me, do you?" Then just chuckle a little bit. It's going to disarm them completely. Sometimes a prospect will respond with "I don't" and they'll hang up on you. But you know what, that's totally cool, man. They weren't for you anyway.

SCHEDULE LIKE A COMEDIAN

You wouldn't think setting a meeting deserves its own section, but it does! Surprise!

A lot of sales reps still have a lot of trouble setting meetings with prospects for some reason. They think of the meeting as something special or precious. They think like, "Oh, I set it. I don't want to touch the prospect again. I don't want to deal with them too much or be too annoying." Many sales reps approach setting the meeting the same way they would approach a date with a person they thought was more attractive than them. That's immediately the wrong attitude to have.

You can't think in terms of setting *a meeting*, you have to think in terms of setting *meetings*. There should be hundreds of meetings you are going to set and your mentality must be "Let's get going. Let's get it rolling." Setting meetings only need a small amount of massaging. Any more than that and it's not worth doing. Above all though, you need a process.

Approach setting a meeting the same way a comedian would approach it. Decide what you are going to do, then just do it. Just have the process, do the thing, and then move on. Give it your best, then detach yourself from the outcome.

When on a call or reading an email reply, as soon as you receive a bit of interest, pull what I like to call this "the Judo move." Judo fighters, they wrestle around standing up and when they feel a little bit of pressure from their opponent they immediately flip their opponent to the mat. You want to think about it like this too; as soon as you get the littlest bit of interest, set the meeting. So, if somebody says "Okay, how would the solution like that work?" That's the reason for the meeting. As soon as they have a question back, as soon as they have the littlest bit of interest, "Who are the people you work with?" Or, "Tell me a little bit more about the people you work with," that becomes the reason for the next meeting. "Great! That's a great idea. You know, I am actually going through a lot of calls right now, but I would love to set a time with you to talk more about it. Let's maybe do this; let me send you an invite for this Friday? We'll talk about it for 20 minutes? I'll send an invite for 30 minutes, but we won't take all that time and we can go from there." Bang! The meeting is set.

Sometimes reps think it's better to actually answer the question right on the phone, but truly, it's better to set the meeting. There are a few reasons why it's better to set the meeting, but a straightforward one is that you can do more with *that* time. On a cold call you're always going to be fighting the clock and any unknown interruptions. A meeting is *protected time*.

The second reason is that setting the meeting actually changes the psychology of the prospect. It's important to understand, but setting a meeting with them is an act of *commission* on their part. By choosing to meet with you they are actually invoking what Robert Cialdini calls in his book Influence "The Commitment and Consistency Principle." If they're agreeing to meet with you then they're *already* moving forward with you toward working together. The thing they wanted to know from you carried them into committing to a meeting from you.

Finally, it's better to set the meeting and have it later because it will allow you *more time* to tailor your pitch to your prospect. No matter how much time you prepared, you won't have all the best preparation at hand while you're cold calling to really put a value prop in front of a prospect. When you set a meeting, you can dive into much more research and put something together that will really make your prospect salivate.

After you set the meeting, stay positive and follow up with something fun and memorable which continues the energy you created on the phone or over email. For example, I set a meeting with a retailer of children's clothing. After looking up the guy I set the meeting with on LinkedIn, I discovered that he actually really likes wine from New Jersey. I had no idea there was such a thing as New Jersey wines. I had no idea that anything but misery grew in New Jersey. Boy was I mistaken. So when I sent a meeting invite to him the meeting I requested said "Brendon and Nino talk about New Jersey wines." He immediately accepted it! He got to the meeting day and said "What is this about New Jersey wines?" I explained to him how I found it, and he went on for the first 10 minutes of the call about New Jersey wine.

That's a lot of rapport that I gained with the prospect very quickly. Some examples of goofy things you can send are "We'll talk about mobile marketing and why Chicago pizza's better," or "Looking forward to chatting with you about the secrets of getting backstage at Imagine Dragons." These are all things I've used before.

If you're really good at this skill, you can actually forward an invite to someone without ever having a conversation with them and get them to accept it. Talking about how to get backstage at Imagine Dragons is something that I sent to the CEO of a company and he accepted it because he loved Imagine Dragons. I saw it from his twitter. Along with the invite I sent a photo of me backstage and Imagine Dragons on stage. He said, "I'll accept this." We talked for a few minutes and he wanted to hear how that happened. After I told him the quick story I pitched him the product and asked who I should speak with at his company about it, he immediately referred me at the end of the meeting.

Make sure that in addition to an agenda in the email you also send some language that relieves pressure on their end. Some language like "Feel free to move this to fit your schedule, I'm going to forward some documentation before hand." Thank them again in the email, and even consider naming qualities you *want* them to have.

This is a big idea, in psychology it's called shaping. It's important, and comedians do it with audiences all the time. Comedians actually reward an audience for who the comedian *wants them to be*. A comedian might say "You guys are so great! Really amazing that you've got an open mind to new kinds of comedy," if they're planning on doing new material.

So, in a sales setting, a sales rep could say "Hey, really appreciate you being open-minded," to a prospect they want to consider something new. Or even more on-the-nose, "Really appreciate you considering all the options." Or "Really appreciate you considering another partner to work with." Or "Even if it doesn't work out, I appreciate you being open-minded." This is rewarding prospects for qualities you *want* them to have. "Can't thank you enough for considering us," is sneaky because nobody really considered you yet, but you can say that and invoke tacit commitment and consistency from the prospect. They *become* the kind of person you want them to be.

You can also refer back to things you might've talked with them about in a previous call. "Man! How crazy was that day that you had? That was amazing. I'm glad you were able to fight for some time and that you thought what I was calling about was valuable enough to give some of it to me." I might say that at the beginning of a phone call, that statement says a lot of powerful things very quickly. Comedians call this a "call back." It pulls the audience back to the relationship that was previously established and it shows a shared history to both parties. That statement above is a call back, it anchors the conversation back to the one we had earlier, and reinforces that I'm someone the prospect was willing to spend time on then, and willing to spend time on now. They can't disagree with the statement because they're clearly *already* in the meeting, they'd have to leave right then if they didn't believe it.

So, here's an assignment: take three prospects of yours right now and think of two reasons why you should meet with them outside of a sales conversation. Take three of them, come up with two reasons for each, that's six altogether. Just outside of a sales conversation, why would you talk to them? If you don't know, then you don't know them well enough to actually prospect them, go do more research.

What you need to understand is that at a certain level of the game in life, transactional relationships are actually *less* valuable because you can have relationships that deliver more than transactional value. Remember, a hundred times a day these three prospects are getting hit up by different people trying to get some of their time. "Hey, check out my thing, it can have value for you." Instead of just doing that, you want to approach connecting in a different way. You want your message to be "Not only could we work together, but outside of that I'm a cool guy, and I will teach you how to get backstage at Imagine Dragons. We're going to talk about the things that you love the most, and we'll talk about a way to actually save your business millions of dollars."

So, this is what you should do. Sit down, think about your prospects, think about two reasons you should talk to them *outside* of just a transactional business conversation.

PERSISTENCE & COMMITMENT

How do you go from good to great? What's the difference between truly world-class performers and everyone else? It's just deciding to do a thing, and then keeping at it. That's it.

In this book we've discussed a lot of things. We've talked about dismissals. We've talked about how comedians handle hecklers. We've talked about all kinds of things—how to structure your day, how to do calls, how to write bits rather than scripts, how to be valuable to other people—but the thing that will take you beyond where you even thought you'd go is simple: It's making a commitment.

Committing to being a high value person who is open to connecting with others and makes things happen, who has their head in the game, shifts your identity and opens you up to entire horizons of success you never thought were possible. When you make that commitment to become that new person, and you recommit to it every day, you will see your life change very powerfully. You'll see your calls changing, getting better, setting more meetings. You'll change the way you even look forward to phone calls, because if you have fun and you commit to being persistently fun on the phone, you *will* have fun. People will have fun with you.

Prospects will have fun with you, and then they'll want to work with you.

Changing the relationship you have to yourself, and then to others is very powerful. Instead of being "The guy who's calling you for a meeting," be, "The guy who's going to meet with you." Do you understand? You're not just calling, "Hey, can I have a meeting?" Or "Hey, I want to talk to you." You're letting them know, "Hey, I'm the guy who's eventually meeting with you." But beyond letting them know, you're letting *you* know that you're the person who's eventually meeting with them.

This doesn't mean being committed to an *outcome*, necessarily. It does mean being committed to pursuing the outcome and only letting go of the outcome if something is really powerfully telling you it's not right anymore. So, if someone says to you on the phone "Listen, we can't work together because my company doesn't do what you are offering value in." That's fine. You don't have to continue pursuing them. In fact, it's probably not worth your time at all. But if you like them, and they're a fun person, just let them know, "Hey, I'm still calling you just because it's fun." I've developed relationships with people that started in a sales setting where I've called the prospect that continue even today, outside of sales, just because I really enjoy talking with them. I'm not trying to sell them something anymore, but they bought into *who I am*. And that's the first step in you selling something to them.

Commit to who you are. Commit to winning for everyone and offering value in your cold calls. Commit to the course that you envisioned reading this book, and the lessons that you're taking from it, then take them on and have success in your cold calling life. Maybe consider getting on stage and telling jokes. It's up to you, life is what you make it, and I would encourage you to do both.

Above all remember the golden rule: Have fun. Because if you're not having a good time, it's probably not worth it anyway.

www.ingramcontent.com/pod-product-compliance
Lightning Source LLC
Chambersburg PA
CBHW030951240526
45463CB00016B/2483